Steps and Missteps

Steps and Missteps

Poems by

Worthy Durgin

My Poetic Pathway Featuring

"Twixt Tick and Tock" &
"Do Caterpillars and Butterflies Ever Kiss?"

Copyright © 2018 Worthy Durgin

ISBN: 978-0-9983676-6-8 (paperback)

LCCN: 2018903180

Printed in the United States

First Edition, 2018

Cover Art Created by: Tully Murray

Poem "Prayers and Meditations for Holy Saturday Scrolls" originally published in e-book "Watching for Easter (Durgin, 2016)

No part of this publication may be reproduced, distributed or transmitted in any form or by any means, including photocopying recording, or other electronic or mechanical methods, without prior written permission of the publisher, except in the case of brief quotations embodied in critical reviews and certain other noncommercial uses permitted by copyright law. For permission requests, write to the publisher at the address below.

With a Capital M Publishing Group, LLC
P.O. Box 52656
Durham, NC 27717
984-244-0793
www.withacapitalm.com
withacapitalm@gmail.com

Special discounts are available on quantity purchases by corporations, associations, and others. For details, contact the publisher at the address above.

Dedicated to:

Roger Manus, Effervescent story teller,
abiding thick and thin friend,
Friday morning sagaciousist.

&

Bennett Myers, Unflinching men's work maven, & a prince, who introduced me to Friday Noon Poets, of Chapel Hill

&

Anita Deters, whose generosity of spirit and spiritual depth have guided my explorations

* * *

I have brought this compendium of poems together in a way that offers thematic threads and narrative for those readers who choose to notice that experience.

If you wish to talk with me about these works, phone conversations can be arranged at Clariity.FM. I look forward to sharing your experience of this work. (May the "zipper" be unbroken.)

Contents

Introduction

Twixt Tick and Tock

Part 1
Human Moments

Steps and Missteps of Life

Reteaching Loveliness

The Myth of Roman Goddess Persnickety and God Punctilious (a minor epic poem)

Water Makes Pictures Bloom

Water Makes a Moment Wilt

Wet Wood Crackles

Purloining Pizza

My Mother's Brother's Bedside

Nature Thrusts and Turns a Sudden Blade

Sagging Sagacity

Manhandling The Truth

The Monarch Butterfly's Journal

Part 2
Divine Aspirations

No Red Convertible for Elijah's Chariot

When the Dervish Spun

The Flame and the Rock

Meditation for Watching for Easter
(from my book: <u>WATCHING for Easter</u>)

Leaning In to Possibility

Thomas Merton Stood Astride

The Triune Self
MY
Personal Resurrection

Living My Gratitude

Part 3
Foolishness

A Leg Man's Lament

Keep Your Fork

The Very Idea

Landslides

Garbled Giblets

Of Lotus and Louts

Atonement Too

Part 4
Tender Engagements

After All

Do Caterpillars and Butterflies Ever Kiss?

Ode to Gregory Ascended

Taking Turns Smoothly

Susan Sings

After the Fall

Boxing Day

Grandparent's Laughing Legacy

Benediction

Introduction

Steps and Missteps

Twixt Tick and Tock

Twixt tick and tock,
Tween boat and dock,
the spaces I create
to find a mate,
in my reader.

What mischief I let loose in our world,
eager for you to fill the voids yourself ?
My pause; pregnant; for your clause.
I invite you in, to your room within,
a full-fledged-flighted fancy
of your own, perhaps.

I love creating that space for meandering meaning,
to molt from my plumage of image
into your chicken coop of cackling mind,
to risk the possibility of being combined
as comfort food, discomfort food, food of the heart-felt hearth.

On the other hand, perhaps as you
read my poem
you become a pinball,
action pinging from image to metaphor,
from near rhyme to knowing,
triggering chimes,
ricocheting about your heart and minds.
Intrigued, you pull the lever,
and launch yourself back into my words
Some balls bounce free, and drain down the
center of the board, Oh well...

Worthy Durgin

Then others are free balls that
go careening through
whatever lapses your synapses enliven -
escaping your own labyrinth's
channel and reward.

Do you ever come back,
to explore my poetic matrix?
Do you start again, creating
a running start at trying to re-connect
the bottom of the front of our shared,
zipper jacket ?

Sometimes, when the magic works,
It is as though the universe
somehow zippered us together;
Arriving at the same conclusion,
surprisingly satisfying,
to both the poem I wrote
and the one you create,
while reading,
in my space,
between.

PART I

Human Moments

Worthy Durgin

Steps and Missteps of Life

1
If one day, my grown daughter could see
the expression I had on my face
that day when she took her first step,
I would be, as happy, as she.

2
Step on a crack... Uprooted, cracked macadam
burgeoning growth along path
and pond breaks open potential
for Mother, earth's come BACK.

3
Skidding across a patina of mud
I greet friends at dawn
with a split hither to unknown to my nethers
a firm earth shake.

4
Strutting gams turn my head
pheromones and lusty groans
six derivative meanings of love
a man's journey below and above.

5
"To love another person
is to see the face of god."
To step in stride, side by side
to welcome, to offer a human guide, a-glide.

Worthy Durgin

6
"Just a closer walk with thee"
Closer than close
I am, They & me;
I am, three.

7
Here I stand
a place to move the world
begins with a single step
I, as Gandhi, choose to march to the sea

8
Had I one chance to employ a wiser man,
with a genie's reset-button,
an anthem I would have learned and sung
each moment, in spite of life, JOY.

9
My diamond jubilee celebrating
playing with my bat and balls;
As I enter my ninth inning, I walk to first,
Eager for extra innings;

Reteaching Loveliness

Galway Kinnell, introduced to me
by Friday Poets in Chapel Hill
on his passing, celebrating:

"...Though sometimes it is necessary
to reteach a thing its loveliness..."

To sit among those gathered,
a pride of 'Friday Noon Poets' poets,
in its 40th year,
kindles in me both un-sparked kindling
and once exhausted embers.

Moments in my creative life
whack-a-moled by events
and responsibilities, over the years,
into yellowed drafts, in attic boxes.

Gratefully re-taught,
I turn to take my turn
in reteaching loveliness
to those who might yet burn.

May I come to enjoy
the blessing of gifting
which Kinnell employed,
with sweet intent, that did not cloy.

Worthy Durgin

The Myth of Roman Goddess Persnickety and God Punctilious
(A Minor Epic Poem about lesser gods)

"I think I am in heaven. Looking down on The
World Series at Shae Stadium! In this fall
sunshine. I feel like a god. It will take Tug
McGraw a while to get ready to pitch. What
you thinkin' so hard on there, boy?"

Grandfather, what does 'white people's time
mean?'
"Oh you must have heard good
ol' Mr. Thorndike gettin' home drunk
and late last night."

Yah, Thorndike said,
"Why were they so damn late for that meeting?
I was there on time.
They should all live
by 'white people's time.'

As mischief twinkled in his wrinkled eye
grandfather paused, smiled, and let his myth
fly.

Years ago, time was slow
Gods Jupiter and Venus
Ruled the show.

Steps and Missteps

There were lesser gods too
who didn't know how to do
but mucked about with me and you.

Punctilious was the god of obsession with time
but then Buddhists spread across the world.
They said — timeless is godliness, holy,
sublime.

People cared less
when to get up and when to get dressed,
a sad day for punctili-'ass.'

And goddess Persnickety insisted everything
done just so

But people 'round the Mediterranean said,
Tis wind and waves tell us how to set sails and
how to go.

When Persnickety and Punctilious felt ignored,
they bothered other gods,
lest they get bored.

Fact is, boy, Jupiter and Venus didn't want
scrutiny when having their fun. Don't tell your
pa I said that, grandson. But I digress...

So Venus and Jupiter made resolution;
Two separate problems needed on solution.
Send them away from heavenly Africa and
Mediterranean.

Worthy Durgin

Then only part of the world shall dwell in
ridged order and anxious time-hell
awaking each morning to the sound of a bell,
and making their bed, "wrinkle free," as well.

Persnickety and Punctilious shall be wed
Venus and Jupiter jokingly said;
It would be fun to watch how tidy they made
THEIR bed.

"Oh grandfather, that's just a story."

"Oh no, boy. You know I stretch my fish. and anyone can stretch the truth, but myths are always true. In fact, they are made to look silly, so that the real truth doesn't scare folks none. Besides, boy, you know what Tug always says about our Mets?"

"You've got to believe!"

"That's right, grandson. That's how some lessor gods get their chosen people. Sometimes, it's a match made in heaven... Now, as I was sayin'... "

Punctilious and Persnickety
wed and then moved that day
up the cold mountains,
where now they hold sway.

Steps and Missteps

And that's why to this very day
the Swiss make precise, punctual watches
as ordered by Punctilious and Persnick-e-tay…

And all the peoples that lived to the north
toiled under their rigor,
for Persnickety and Punctilious,
they were the god-boss.

"That's why those folks make love like
someone is watchin' them from over their
lover's butt, when the have their fun. (Don't
tell your grandmother I said **that**, grandson."

To praise goddess Persnickety,
to this VERY day
Those poor folk make their watches say
"tick tick ticki-tay"

What do they say to praise god Punctilious?
Up the Matterhorn,
their voices climb,
"They should all live by white people's time!"

"Gee Grandfather,
I feel sorry for those folk,
after all."

A smile of satisfaction
swelled grandfather's wrinkled cheek.
And far below on the baseball field,
the umpire yelled, "Play Ball!"

Worthy Durgin

Steps and Missteps

Water Makes Pictures Bloom
(Sarah's gift)

Watering my camera
so we can 'grow more pictures,'
my daughter greets my visiting sister
from the far coast.

A three year old connects dots
that make so much sense;
she knows I want to make pictures,
and is so helpful.

The water from the hose
splashes playfully on the lens
panic grows
turning away, from friends.

Worthy Durgin

**Water Makes Moments Wilt
(a father's lament)**

In a moment of distraction,
family conviviality is shattered
by not instantly understanding
the metaphor of
a little girl's, loving intention.

When an extra piece of cake
simply does not suffice,
One can only lament,
how the Grand Canyon
was created in such a gut wrenching instant.

No bridge can span
the joy, torn asunder.
Cries sound like thunder,
unbearable to the paternal ear.
"Please don't go, my dear."

The Wet Wood Crackles

The wet wood crackles
the thick piney smoke
full of musk that middle aged men wish
their bodies still effused.

Now, apart from their daily lives,
they drum and thump and cry con-effused,
shouting their manhood on retreat,
until they almost assure each other
that they are
who they dream themselves might be.

Years into gender shifts of '60's and '70's men
sought definition and meaning
they could stand fore-square —
without anyone correcting
their masculinity or their grammar.

Confidence seeking together,
that they could withstand confusion,
guilt, fear, condemnation;
from women whose rain-bow reached as wide
a spectrum as the Orange juice saleswoman:
exhorting men to rule the marriage - - to Bell-
Absugging, hat wielding, bonnet-burning
libbing.

Sleepless nights of bugs and dew and
brothers-too? This is a thirsted respite?
Actually, yes. In that time, God, yes.
Behold a great notion,
a story of stories

Worthy Durgin

Jungians reaching deep
in their archetypal ballsack
to bridge that gap with
scores of metaphors.

Striving to find an aspect of manhood
beyond assault,
Bly and Campbell and many others
sought an unassailable essence,
preferably from petroglyphs, the myths,
the historically dustier the better,
essence of tribal men
from primitives.
they found 'INITIATION.'

I "matured" among men
from Madison Avenue,
who molded male meaning
in 60 second impressions —
bold, dynamic, roost-ruling,
unafraid of cigarette hastened death,
in the driver seat of every new car.
Advertisement relationships.

But in their own silence on the weekend,
myth provided ambiguity, at the very least.
And by the time they had discussed men's
work sufficiently,
often with the same men,
there was sufficient kindling
burning in
"authentic" interactions among men

Steps and Missteps

That it was its own refuge,
sufficient to absorb
the whiplashing impact
of daily, gamey grind.

Now, 30 or 40 years on,
those men shared the stories
and the rituals they created.
The hormones
that hallmarked their bonding
faded as their vision, their hearing, their vigor
of railing into the ember filled night.
The dying flames too vivid a metaphor.

Now the men sought young to be Jung men;
men who could live their memories for them.
They sought young men
to honor their being elders,
even as they once re-birthed each other
into adult manhood
with intentions of other initiations.
Where are these young Jung men,
once again beckoned by gender wars
of such chilling intensity
that it would shrink the gonads?

Yet, today, as if sensing an existential need,
the universe has unleashed 'ME TOO.'
**Perhaps this societal realignment
will create new men who seek their
footing on solid mythic earth.**

Worthy Durgin

If, young man,
you hear crackling wood
beyond the glade,
come hither.
Come be men with us;
**for our salvation
and, perhaps, your own,
lies in your *would*.**

Steps and Missteps

Purloining Pizza

Leading the charge
down Philmont mountains
my Happy Eagle son
purloins pizza for his pioneers
at the sunset of a week-long adventure.

I was not a scout,
and I missed my father.
I tried so hard to be
a good Eagle's father,
and I missed my son.

I never woke to the dawn
that a *good* sitcom
can be the training video
for family connections
of shared life.

Joy-filled doing and being in daily life
accepting, uplifting in spite of
the fullness life presents
fixing the tire together,
or purloining the pizza.

Worthy Durgin

My Mother's Brother's Bedside

*'Please consider
PEACE
in each personal
choice you make
each day.'*

So says my sign.
But even this day,
some one of this witnessing group
will choose to hold my aunt's sign,
channeling her unstinting commitment;
honoring her compassion.

Here I stand, in front of
the main post office, on the
420th *consecutive* first Wednesday.
A monthly resurrection
of the dove of peace
for these weathered souls.

My sign next to hers,
in a relay of
35 years, over 30 witnessed
by uncle and aunt
Against war, a war economy,
Against nuclear weapons,
for peace and humanity's wellbeing.

To stand in their footsteps,
like standing amid
four prior generations
in the cemetery of

Worthy Durgin

Springfield Meeting House,
is to know some slight power of totem,
some gift of gene-pool
for which I am rich,
this day or that.

What torch would you choose to lift
from the hand of one who matters,
that would matter to them and to you,
that would matter enough
for you to stoke that flame?

That day near parting
I sat quietly with him.
He sipped a spoon of lobster bisque,
to his nurse's surprise.
My mother's brother and I
talked of this and that.

The next day I sat, silently with him,
as he bestowed unspoken volumes of
tomorrows to me.
I listened, and I wrote.
I seemed hear….

Peace is the meaning
of his sound being,
of his faltering breath;
his backhand quiet at his side,
his top spin no longer
jumping up with surprise.
Beyond stillness and quiet,

peace is his fashion,
peace, his passion.

Even quiescent acquiescence
his courageous slipping,
passing into my heart.
Peaceful passing, with understanding.

All those I have known
giving so generously
of their time,
their love's energy;
to B E for others, to learn
to sustain, that others might thrive,
to share time with me, alive;
I am so rich for them.

Can you imagine
how much worse
it might have been,
had we not stood?
Stand, while you can.

Ever had I the wherewithal
to lift up something in his honor,
what might that be?
"Peace," he breathed, at his end.

Worthy Durgin

Nature Thrusts and Turns a Sudden Blade

Just yesterday
the short sleeved picnic at Lake Johnson
was so balmy and bright, my friend
had to have her wheelchair repositioned,
so she would not get too much sun.

The fowl glided onto the soft, indigo water
separated from the azure sky by a fiery belt
of confligratory colors, of
leaves celebrating a life well spent.

Tonight the ducks may have to check their
landing spot for ice
as they descend into the first biting freeze.
So drastic, so early this sudden icy blade,
thrust outrageously just
two weeks before Carolina Thanksgiving.

Worthy Durgin

Sagging Sagacity

The slip between the cup and the lip
allows a poem to drip
down my chin
between my whiskers.
Down to posterity;
Are they thirsty?

Will they catch it,
possible wisdom in a poem,
like a foul ball
giddy when life-long empty gloves
are finally stuffed with leather and string?

Or will taste and times dictate disinterest?
Generations tone deaf to
'Twixt, Tick and Tock'?
Sounds of a millennial clock,
handles and lost to digital space,
a typed word lost from
Gothenburg trace.

'Twixt tweet and Text,
Tween now and next,'
Really?
Not so much,
I hope.

Manhandling The Truth

My then wife would say
*women dress for other women,
NOT for men.*
Poppy COCK.

There comes, for some men,
a time when
they grow the three day beard
not to woo women with stubbled pheromones,

But to anticipate being
on a weekend retreat with other men
to anticipate standing in a man's truth
to shout their poems across the camp fire
to scratch and spit into the fire pit
of masculinity manhandling the truth
in wounded, healing exultation.

They say women dress for other women.
Maybe, sometimes;
it's true.

Worthy Durgin

The Monarch Butterfly's Journal**

The butterflies about me seem like me.
They soar on thermals, high in the trees.
They savor stamen nectars
flavored differently.

Yet, the other butterflies look at me,
'Why do you always go that way, northerly?'
Sometimes they teasingly glide southerly
I think to taunt me, for me to realize
what my direction must always be.

While I have heard that butterflies are free,
while I travel alone ore field and tree,
I must admit my choice always seems to be
by choice or by nature, northward proclivity.

Ahead, on the horizon a vast blue sea
Neither flower nor field can I see
yet I press on, across lake Huron, inexorably
drawn by a "purpose" "greater than me?"

Which is more precious —
"posterity's purpose," or being "free?"
Which me, would I rather be?
A challenging question , for a loner, to see
A disappointing answer, for a loner to see.

Worthy Durgin

*Of a Monarch Butterfly on the third leg of the northward migration, before the fifth generation returns to 30 square mile area in Mexico- 2,000 miles away, at year's end, to start again.

PART 2

Divine Aspirations

Worthy Durgin

When THIS Dervish Spun

Survivor, Provider, Defender
However bumpy
Soul's heart path
Soared above,
there was that time when this dervish spun.

When this bear
stumbled our of my cranial hibernation
comfortable in certain connections
hid from fault
choosing survival as sufficient
there was that time,
when this bear lumbered.

Striding open-hearted
beyond enough,
into open possibilities
this moment the mortar
my intention the pestle;
grinding a mustard seed
to flavor my life as a sharing,
I now create this third time
my soul heart-path progressing.

Steps and Missteps

No Red Convertible for Elijah's Chariot

Culture be damed,
human nature may reach beyond
fashion and convention.

For Merton and Rohr
life holds more than
managing the mundane.

The true self awaits
a person's discovering traits
as deep as truth, as true as soul.

Stumbled into, in total surrender
of mid life realities,
they offer The True Self.

I posit that this,
God's Gift to each person
Is too precious to be left hidden.

Time is too short, Truth too precious
to leave to chance of
a mid-life dance.

We can help you grow now
we can lift you grow now
you may can choose to grow somehow.

Worthy Durgin

I bid you watch and see, notice and grasp,
each glimpse of thy True Self.

Clutch it to your breast as a girl's diary
as truly you and uniquely true
memorize the texture of its touch.

Make yourself as fully whole
as you can, now; and now again
and again growing in full humanity.

Imagine a flaming chariot
burning in your breast
cleansing the rest, for living your best.

You, Elijah,
step into your chariot
and connect the divine with the sublime.

By the time you need a red convertible,
it may have an electric motor.
Why wait for that?

Steps and Missteps

The Flame and the Rock

*By the time I experience the flame
it has already moved
sometimes flickered into godless yearning
sometimes inspiring a blaze of blessing*

*The rock "on which"
seemingly solid and sure
Spirit in my life
unflinchingly insecure
I AM*

*Wrenched from institution and conflict
flame licks persistently into crevices of fear
The solid and the etherial / ephemeral
entwined
whists of doubt vanquished with hope, in faith*

*Break forth from ambered-tradition's tomb
in assurance of time
a moment sufficient for spiritual
eruption?*

*How direct one can connect
Scriptural omissions
and church commissions,
chains of rusted links
turned to dust.*

Worthy Durgin

A high cheek smile
solid and ephemeral at once,
faith entrusts;
spirit persists;
it is;
I AM.

Steps and Missteps

Prayers and Meditations for Holy Saturday Scrolls

*Each item is both
a stand alone prompt for
meditation and prayer,
and one step along
the arc from Good Friday evening
to Easter dawn:*

*This is the last day of Lent.
There is still the opportunity
      to "give something up for Lent"
Might I possibly choose
to give up for Lent,
now, any sense of
estrangement from God?*

*I hold GOD's eternal flame,
      alive and healing in my Heart.
It flickers, but never wavers.
Thanks B E to God.*

*By the time I see the flame,
it has already changed.
so quickly may my heart
change and know resurrection.*

Worthy Durgin

*May I cleanse and recommit myself
in preparation of the Easter Party,
such that I am not just an observer,
I am a participant, in divine resurrection.*

*Forgive me God,
if even a moment's denial of You, by me,
causes you the slightest anguish,
such as that of Good Friday.*

*Knowing and rejoicing
that I am forgiven of God,
may I forgive myself,
so that I may walk closer with God.*

Leaning in to Possibility

Watching is neither the beauty of inflection
nor Wallace Stevens' innuendoes
just after the blackbird whistles:

Watching is like baited breath on a spring day,
silently leaning in to hear the anticipated call;
pregnant expectation,
a yearning for the renewed connection with
the blackbird's whistle.

Watching asks, how can I best tilt my head
to listen, to hear, to relish the inflection;
how can I open my heart to comprehend
what the brain can only trifle;
How can I position my feet to most efficiently
step forth in the world in be-loving response.

Watching is a personal experience of
being birthed afresh with Christian possibility.

Worthy Durgin

Thomas Merton Stood Astride

Thomas Merton Stood Astride
gulfs between millennia of Christian practice
and contemporary orthodoxies

Thomas Merton stood astride
valleys slouching 'tween
Christendom and other traditions

Thomas Merton stood astride
costly, rage-filled fears
of habit and open prayer

Encouraged to publish, he did not parish.
He stood not aside but astride.

+ + +

Even now Merton's open doubts create space
for Hiroshima, Holocaust post-livers
to catch their breath in prayer,
and hope it was not they who have died
to the possibilities of ... God's peace.

So many had died;
now, so many tried,
tortured in the easy sound of
Paul Simon's "Sounds of Silence"
belying despair,
space in a cloistered cell to hope and dare,
that we might still care,

Steps and Missteps

So many traditions, even
technologies to trigger
"The God mind" electronically,
there's no less the divide
in which to hide
in debates and accusations,
epithets of heresies abide

A mere 50 years on
God's timeless invitation
still share,
even oddly,
in this mystic's prayer.

Directionless guidance from
God's still voice?
Thank goodness
Merton did not stand aside.

Worthy Durgin

The Triune Self

*Merton and Rohr share appellation of
personal bifurcation
Two parted self, false self and true
healthy real parts of a healthy you.*

*"False" seems pejorative, beyond intention
"Mundane" more clear, without sensation
Work-a-day, you alive in creation
well entwined in Christian's good station.*

*Unlike Tao and Buddhist objective
Christian's pursuits is to be active
to work God's will through prayerful insight
in this volition one seeks to "B E" right*

*God created human kind
in the image of God.
Our Triune God making humans
persons in three persons?*

God creator, the mundane self
God the spirited, the true self
Living action in Christ's example
parallel interesting, seems more than ample.

But, need we be old with beards of gray?
Never that, I pray.

Steps and Missteps

Youth be served
Youth of service be
Youth's cradle crucible
Youth Do and B E

Mundane Self
True Self
Triune Self
Create, and B E, and Act, as one

Then blossoms as one, the trinity
fully human but divinely inspired
acting as Jesus

Asserting capability
while defined by the mystery
sustained in all facets
Thanks B E with God

Worthy Durgin

My

The word says it all
My car; my book; my father
It is not him
It is my perception; creation; concoction

It's alive, it's alive, it's alive
Thus spake Frankenstein
after jolting his super-man cadaver to
"rebirth."

I jolt my cadavers to life
with expectations, disappointments,
and even congratulations.
I bring them to life as
the person I require them to be.

Perhaps I should recall Frankenstein as
an unsympathetic figure
when I, like God,
I have created "My"

In "My" own image.

The only creation I create is distance.
separation between me
and the other I create.

Does God ever realize that same forsake?
Perhaps They are the Trinity
to overcome that original,

Steps and Missteps

perhaps that is THE original mistake.

Perhaps my Triune Self,
created in Triune God's image,
offers a best chance to
reconnect in divine relationships.

B E-*ing*, *Doing*, and acting in Christ manner
Re-birthing all relationships;
with my many selves,
and all my others,

Lazarus
realized,
I pray,
I rise.

Worthy Durgin

*Personal Resurrection into Our Triune Self**

We alight from that tomb
of the dominating mundane,
into awareness sunshine
anchored in our True Self;
Realized in the healthy,
whole-person balance
of Mundane** and True Selves.
May we stride forth,
Our Triune Self,
in divine balance,
to B E & to do,
a mission of God.

*This poem was created and sent as a thank you gift to Richard Rohr, Monk of the Order of Saint Francis Reviewer of my previous book, "WATCHING for Easter".

**The construct of "B E-ing and Doing" are central to that book and to life as I have grown to appreciate it.
.

Living My Gratitude

There are so many Souls who spark
  one's heart along the path.
The light swells one's daybreak sky;
  the heat warms on through.
Gratitude etching lines on
  the pilgrim's pathway.
Coming forth from one's own tomb
  with service mission joy.
Easter dawn vitality.

Worthy Durgin

Part 3

Foolishness

Steps and Missteps

A Leg Man's Lament
(leering on the edge)

The hunks of High Point's
Firemen's Calendar
agitate and titillate
even women
of a 'me too' generation.

Speaking of calendars,
Have you noticed,
The word "G A M S"
no longer graces
our civilization's lexicon.

I had to add "gams"
to my computer dictionary
today,
just for this poem.

One of the visions
that spurred our troops
to victory in World War II,
no longer accessible, as acceptable.

Oh, we can see more leg than ever,
"a little ankle"
now stands in the dust
of time.

Worthy Durgin

Left far below the heightened hem
left far too low,
beneath high volumed appetites,
whispered more softly
than the touch of a thigh
so not to offend liberated so-ciet-y.

Hem four inches above the knee
scandalized if admired gawkingly;
what is it she shows all to see
a millennial woman of liberty?

Perhaps if they were clad in silk,
gams soothed and tingled as she walks,
she would enjoy her gams enough to share,
even with men, who love to stare.

The men on calendar pages
understand, as all have for ages,
how a certain gal might
conjure a Fireman's photo tonight.

Keep Your Fork

You are welcome to more
easy welcome guest
easy welcoming host
ample food is best
hospitality galore.

Lightly bantered repartee
nothing boorish or dull
what subjects left one can explore
rattle round a convivial skull
for all who partake

You will find at book's end
pancakes that stretch
as far as generations
of college students have etched,
hungry for life and for friend.

10,000 forks for you and more
to keep for the next
who care less for form
for true life are vexed
not near rhyme or metaphor.

Worthy Durgin

Landslides

Landslides

D
  O
    W
     N

Sandy mountains

     e r
   v   i
 o   n
c   g

  my feet

A beach in heat.

The Very Idea

An idea is an Arab
on a white stallion
charging across
the desert of the mind.

An idea is a chef's unique omelet
presented to a glutinous man,
who considers savoring it,
then rests it idly on his belly.

An idea crashes
through the brambled woods
into the campsite, growling,
I am a bear, so there.

An idea is a turtle,
freshly hatched amongst
thickets and twisted old vines,
sloping down the bank
into the murky ebb and flow.
Too much bother to finish
in just four, short lines.

An idea
plays peek-a-boo
late at night
in vast silences of apnea.

Worthy Durgin

An idea jumps like popcorn
over the flame in the fireplace
against the stifling wall of medication,
or did I mean meditation?

An idea enforces my obligation to
my father's, father's father
that I should pretend
he was right in the first place.

An idea soars about the room
like a brilliant balloon
just out of the reach
of a crying child.

An idea is a bulb
that comes up amid daffodils
and spreads her feminine wiles sensuously
to purr, "I am an Iris."

Steps and Missteps

I invite you to use this space to write your own thoughts and/or metaphors of *an idea...*
-

Worthy Durgin

Of Lotus and Louts

Reading a poem aloud,
to my poet's' gathering,
I suddenly misread a word.
Instead of "Lotus,"
I misread it as "Louts."

To the poem or the group, had I been rude?
I vowed then and there to make all square
by writing a poem
including both a 'lotus' and a 'louts.'

Herewith, food for thought:

Worthy Durgin

Garbled Giblets

Remembering the lesson
of the lotus and the louts,

Upon receiving a summons
for Thanksgiving gouts,
a festive gathering
of an awakened gaggle,
Vegetarian, vegan, or turkey to gobble?

I replied in a parlance that all would know:
"As a lone wolf, I will go with the ... *fowl.*"

Steps and Missteps

Atonement Too

Oblivious to the spiritual sublimity,
the louts trod through the bog
rather than notice the lotus.

Worthy Durgin

PART 4

TENDER ENGAGEMENTS

After All

It is, after all,

Only in hindsight,

That one can make up a story,

About whether a given stride

Was a step or a misstep.

Most often, it is both.

Worthy Durgin

Do Caterpillars and Butterflies Ever Kiss?

In the dim mood-lighting
of their common chrysalis
Do caterpillars and butterflies ever Kiss?

Is there a moment
or even an instant
when a circular breath of
expiring and inspiring commingles?

Do they exchange DNA in
a blissful moment of coital unraveling
passing batons of life information and
regenerative purpose / passion?

There is much ado about how the caterpillar
must surrender life, never know the beauty it
will have wrought.

That, exhausted from building the cocoon,
there is naught to de done
than to be undone,
legs and fir and senses slop into a decay.

Yet we know, the decay is genuinely primordial
ooze
soup that gives clues
and begins to bubble and froth
into the being that will flutter aloft.

Worthy Durgin

Methinks there is more
in that caldron
than bubble and trouble.

In this stew there is glue of connection
one state to another
like for us perhaps, a brief time of
"brightening,"
prelude to that last sigh,
that time of awareness that,
it is accomplished, indeed;
and that striding forth into
a new you awaits.

Realizing the profound creativity
of that experience
our caterpillar-self can pass that baton of
ethereal DNA
not with gentle good night,
but with GUSTO

Having known the fullness of "L'cheim" life
and sending our essence forth
like christening a ship with
the effervescence of exploding champagne,
a different sort of caldron bubble
a bliss of death that proclaims, TO LIFE.

Let each day be a *petite mort*
of such sublimity
May you morph excitedly
From last year's accomplished caterpillar
to next year's beautiful butterfly.
Greet each day, as your re-birth day!

Steps and Missteps

Ode to Gregory Ascended

Gregory loved the breath into the dawn
Raspy suggestions of a tune
struggle through the soup
of low hung fog or early dew.
At first the single tent
in the swale of rocky road and long leaf pine
clouds the tone to all
but those lucky enough to be sleepless
in the graying black of pre morning.

Gregory alights from his tent
as light tells him time has arrived
to summon brothers to unplug ears,
do morning pee, and stumble wearily
out of cabins. Chilly dew reminds them
to clutch sleepy arms over shirts.
No one speaks, nearly a throat is cleared,
as piper tune "pipes" with song,
summoning men
to circumambulate in peaceful,
mindful, paces.

Gregory casts his eye
to monitor his soft soft
barefooted steps mindfully
on the weeds, gravel, and clay
of the path he trods wearily, annually
on the retreat's dawning days.

He is fully in and universally beyond
his background
his dreadlocks claim his groundedness,

Worthy Durgin

Even as he affords others
open hearted welcome,
to meet him open hearted, thither.

Wait, is Gregory
in the present or in the past tense?
Yes. Tense loses relevance
for a timeless soul;
connecting at once, with both now and then.

Gregory has allowed the music
to induce me to scratch a verse.
I've not been here before;
I do not realize I can
share that verse at trail's end
before we join our coffee-first brethren,
'round breaking fast and storied re-past.

The day is fully begun before the sun
answers Gregory's siren's call and
nudges up over the hilly horizon
and shoulders its way through
the soup of low hung clouds or early dew.

This dawn, this year, years hence,
I circle the lake where he once led.
A memorial bench
heralds the sitting space.

Steps and Missteps

The wood of this special bench,
where his picture greets new generations,
is of a 700 year-old cypress.
What better sense of timelessness
of his presence
could loving brothers testimony share
to anyone opening there?

Gregory's countenance *is* everywhere,
and love,
and care;
graces my day's
joining with others around,
as he would be,
welcoming.

I still sense the sound of
Gregory's loving the breath into the dawn,
of each moment that I am
conscious and present,
when living my song.

Thank you Gregory.

Worthy Durgin

Kathy Taking Turns Smoothly

Blueberry, Blueberry. Blueberry pancakes
That's the turning cadence within to sing
beach music's dance of east coast swing

Releasing your focus
beyond your partner's mane,
Suddenly, easily, you see the same
ballroom from a new outlook
on life's chapter-ed book.

My now passed friend
taught me patiently,
before her time to turn,
when it was not her turn.

And as that time swung close,
I suggested lovingly,
glide smoothly across your path, toning
transition, transition, transition smoothly...

Look back into this, our ballroom, briefly
then twirl girl, to the light and music
of your new dance hall.
Tis, but a blueberry ball.

Susan Sings

Festooned fortifications,
spread like a Las Vegas buffet
herbs, tinctures, supplements,
a cornucopia of passion for life.

Beyond fueling life's appetites,
the spread buttressed her, against assaults,
a cacophony of cells, cysts and tumors.
She, herself a phalanx
against her body's rebellion.

Beyond her years
of given hope and expectations
Her smile;
she might have taught the Cheshire cat.

Lusty, full throat-ed *joie de vivre,*
still bursting through
her skin in indomitable freckles,
she is grateful for friends who come,
finally to share, her choice to leave.

Worthy Durgin

After the Fall

My dog
flinches in his dream
by the winter hearth
when an ember explodes.

Puppy dog sleep eyes
look up at the ceiling wearily
perhaps remembering
the attack of the acorns.

Maybe that moment when
he leaped full-stride,
in summer's full throttle,
catching the frisbee's banking return
from its launching and
received a barrage of acorns
on a tender snout.

Awakened ones are quick to say
animals live in the moment,
why don't we, like they?

Ask my dog why his snout hurts
when an ember pops on a winter's day.
We are, after all,
as mindful, as they.

Boxing Day

Part One
All She Wants for Christmas

Each year the pile in the corner
seemed to grow taller for her,
even as the size of the balsam fir
appearing in the living room corner
of her childhood home,
always stretching to the ceiling.
But shrinking with years.

Now, too uncertain to walk her way
through the boxes herself,
she was there on a chillier day
than she would have chosen
Twelve days after Labor Day,
this year's "boxing day."

A day when the young fellow
from church was available,
after chess club and
before his basketball game that
evening,
to help her unearth her things
from the winter corner of her unit.

Worthy Durgin

Atop the winter box corner of the
storage
was the red box.
She could see with both eyes and her
heart
the green piping on the box was un-
frayed.

The red canvas cover, sadly unsullied,
without
stains of gingerbread fingers
rifling through ornaments
to create the most wonderful tree, ever.

the fact this box was atop
a stack of brown and white storage
boxes
was her testament to Christmas hope.

The young man moved
with amazing grace, in her eyes
nutcrackering with bends and bobbs
(almost effortlessly), as he moved this
table to reach that box, to lift it down,
or carry it outside to reach deeper,
into the unit, as into her past.

next, rummaging among the garden boxes
- does bagged dirt ever expire?
- how many years had it boon since she canned?
- would steaks uphold beefsteak tomatoes
ever, again?

The kitchen pots were still boxed
for that someday kitchen,
when she would not have to pay
to restock her apartment
with utensils or such things
needed to bake gingerbread cookies
for hoped for grandchildren.

The red box above winter togs,
and covers, and even boots
would she dare use boots,
if there were snow on the ground?

The box placed before her
atop the step stool
she began through the box
un-layering the years
while he began repacking

the other seasons
into the empty corner.

Part Two:
Being Naughty

Through a heavy sigh
of the task ahead,
summoning hope
she spotted the legend on the back
of the young man's shirt

"What does it say?

Transylvania Cascades

"Are those the waterfalls
in Transylvania County?
Years ago... My husband and I
used to love seeing them
in the summer.
Is that what brings you joy?"

"I like to discover them.
I like to see them too.
But I really like to find them.

far up in the leafless hills, where the
topographic lines hug each other", he
replied.

"Topogra…", Her memory interrupts
his line of conversation.
"It was the thunder… and the spray
that he and she reveled in, in her day.
The ache in her calves as her husband's
powerful grip pulled her up to the next
mossy pool. Exhilarated, sometimes,
they would get naughty in the shrubs.

Waterfall, mountains…
her blood surges like fountains…
but really only slightly
more throbbing in her hands.
Her smile evaporates
like waterfall mist.

She regards the box-filled storage unit
and the red box he has placed before
her.

Part Three
Her Days of Christmas Past

She sat in that so distinctive chair -

Worthy Durgin

the icon of her used-to-be living room,
now by the entrance to the unit,
Her freshly auburned hair
flickering like flames.
out from beneath a tattered scarf
against the chilly breeze

Someday she would be doing this
by the toasty warmth of
her again very own fireplace hearth
embraced by a one-sided warming,
woolen shawl, perhaps with grand-
youngins 'round her...

she lifted the lid of the red box on the
step stool
and began to look at the ornaments she
would
once-again-choose-not-to-put-out
in her apartment this year

1
After all these years, paper rings on top,
so not to be crushed; she smiled
remembering
how each of the family took turns
adding the next link in the paper chain
year after year, sometimes with a note...
Hers were the yellow rings.

2
A tiffany blue disk with white snow flake
on the back 1971
their first Christmas.

3
One does not fill one's own stocking,
she put this one back,
in the side space in the box.

4
A clear crystal inscribed with "*PEACE*"
a yearning for their shared souls
after their ungodly loss that year.

5
A disk with an image of a boy
with protruding toddler's tummy
her second son's first Christmas,
two years later.

6
Six inch elongated, alabaster,
be-glittered father Christmas,
that always accentuated
the biggest gap in that year's boughs.

7
A cut-out brass fire place
four stockings were hung
their daughter's first Christmas.

8
It had been a rough year
when they bought this peace ornament.
For the world and themselves,
it was a prayer.

9
Pull the string at the elf's bottom
and his arms and legs fly out sideways,
in time with all the fart noise
competition among the giggling kids.

10
Creche of drinking straw roof
and painted cardboard figures.
…maybe if she could put
some chewing gum behind the figures
to hold them upright,
it would come to life again.

11
Remembering finding the kind of glue to make
the white felt skirt stay in place

on the white plastic spoon
with the gold-dipped
pipe cleaner halo - what an angel.

The other boxes are all back in place.
Now she lets the young man put the lid
back on this last box.

Like a little boy,
privileged to place the star
atop the great balsam fir
in the living-room,
he reaches to the tip top of the pile of
boxes in the corner of the storage unit
and replaces the box of decorations
till next she comes.

Part Four
Creating Christmas

As the box regains its rightful place
in the upper corner of the unit,
a chapter is closed.
This ritual has kindled and rekindled
many forms of flame in
her always-mending heart.
She determinedly turns her heart

Worthy Durgin

from dusty boxes to her now traditional
twelfth day of Christmas.

She stands a bit unsurely. The long sit
in the chair, the damp chill in the
September air has stiffened her joints.
Her step emboldened,
she lengthens her gate.

This day fuels so many ideas,
like dancing sugar plums,
of what joys she will bring,
to many friends, old and new
to warm their holidays this year.
The twelfth day
will be the days ahead
she creates for others.

Her heart engine humming purposely,
she looks forward to the world's boxing
day at new year's beginning.

Grandparents' Laughing Legacy

SHE: A mayor's daughter
of a man forever repaying
money partner absconded,
now married to a mission

HE: Quaker church too small
for son of a world-traveling
missionary, now a mission person &
life-long community gardener.

SHE: Dancing her finger piano keys,
Joy in their heart revelries.
10,000 pancake meals for
guests on Sundays, if you please.

HE: Creating-community.
Crafting his solutions,
a student sleeping in a broom closet
to learn enough
to become a doctor,
who, 70 years later,
lives re-hospital-ity.
by telling me of grandparents
who changed lives.

Worthy Durgin

THEY: Generous for generations
Through 20s that roar,
depression and war
then the fifties galore;
mission to students
hospitality, what for?

Surely the experience itself
Yes, but what more?
To teach generations
hospitality of receiving
by exampling
the hospitality of giving.

Generations of young men.
now paying forward pancake ken
now paying forward the generosity,
of JOYful piano key singers
with tunes of their own times.

Are there 'pancakes' in these pages?
Are their songs in these lines?
Is there JOY in one's heart?
Has the reading been fine, sometime?

What of your now opportunities
your soul to let shine?
What of God in you,
may others see as sublime?

Steps and Missteps

Steps or missteps
can hardly matter
when mindful heart mind
lifts a day new and greater.

~~ * ~~

Remember our beginning
'tween this' and 'twixt that?'
You've done rather well,
throughout to have sat.

Thank you for being
my unzipped-zipper-upper.
Thanks for coming
to this open-house supper.

And if you would chat
'bout this or 'bout that,
Clarity FM is where I'll be at.

Worthy Durgin

Benediction

The sun sets
behind the hills.
Passions rest
with put down quills.
Daybreak stirs action;
go B E, go Do,
whatever your faction,
Blessings on You.

Steps and Missteps

Appendix

Appendix A

About the Author

Mr. Worthy Durgin was most fortunate to earn his Masters of Divinity at Yale, while Henri Nouwen was on that faculty. His own focus on hospital chaplaincy and counseling has shaped his life in many ways.

Durgin's career has ranged from running a psychiatric half way house to running the South Street Seaport Museum in NYC. Throughout the 1990s, he led a fledgling community foundation in Greensboro North Carolina. Assets grew 10 fold, even while developing its engaged mission.

The past 15 years have been a time of deeply personal, spiritual awakening and practice. He and his family now live in Raleigh. A key aspect of this period has been deep "men's work." Mr. Durgin alludes to this growth in a number of these poems. The Mankind Project, The Triangle Men's Center, and the North Carolina Gathering of Men have been important influences. The relationships with men who strive to be authentic, however, have made the biggest differences.

These eclectic experiences are reflected in the wide variety of groups with which he enjoys presenting and discussing his work.

~ * ~

Steps and Missteps is Durgin's first compendium of poetry. For those who choose to read it straight through, there are rewarding threads to be discovered in juxtapositions and sequences of life lessons

Appendix B

Other Works by the Author

Morning Glory: A collection of short stories and associated reflections, will be published next year. Mr. Durgin has told these true personal stories in a variety of venues. He shares these personal events with candor. His approach entices the reader to open their own hearts just as wide, in connecting very personally, as they reflect "together" on personal life paths.

~ * ~

WATCHING: is a trilogy of books which focuses on Easter, as both a series of events, and as a metaphor. It is an opportunity for actively preparing oneself for "personal resurrection." The program is an ecumenical approach to deeply Christian faith.

These 3 books stem from a 24 hour vigil he created for Holy Saturday at White Memorial Presbyterian Church in Raleigh, in 2016.

WATCHING for Easter is the first book in the series. It provides the content of the vigil. The process of creating this 24 hour vigil was a profound opening to leaders' faith. The one hour segments, including some of the actual scripts, invited to see the time after Good Friday as a period for very active personal preparation to participate in Easter.

The book explores, in depth, that understanding "B E-ing and DO-ing" has significant meaning for Christians exploring their spirituality. The vigil, in its entirety prepares one to prepare oneself to participate actively in Easter, rather than to simply" observe it."

Other books in this series that are in the offing:

The Trinity:

Three Windows
One light
God

WATCHING: B E-*ing* Spiritually Vigilant provides six distinct ways of exploring the themes of the vigil in different formats. These formats ranges from abbreviated vigils, to a Lenten study, to a year-long books study. Vigil scripts are included.

Some of the approaches include individual and group contemplative practices. In this photo from the cover of the book, a person is walk a labyrinth in the chapel.

The three clear windows in the chapel were the inspiration for a meditation I brought to our weekly contemplative prayer group. My phrase, leading to 20 minutes of silent meditation, focuses on

~ * ~

NIMBILITY: This Man's Next First Step is the third book in the WATCHING series. It focuses on how churches can nurture and sustain personal spiritual growth within Christian faith tradition.

Christians need not leave the fellowship of their own church to follow spiritual calling. And churches can grow stronger by embracing these aspects of faith as well as embracing church members who are opening spiritually.

For example, one imagines that a *tight rope walker knows precisely where she is going and chooses when to start. On a spiritual journey, a pilgrim opens to the path when moved, without knowing where any single step in faith may lead. Each step IS a leap of faith. Each step IS that person's "next first step."*

<u>Nimbility</u> helps the reader understand such a pilgrim's experience. It sheds light on the experience of the one who lives it. It also elucidates what is happening for those family and friends, who want to know how to embrace and support their loved one's experience, within their Christian home.

To learn more about the author, speak with directly, and/or book him for your next event:

Clarity.fm/worthydurgin

worthydurgin.com

www.ingramcontent.com/pod-product-compliance
Lightning Source LLC
LaVergne TN
LVHW051847080426
835512LV00018B/3112